10 Things I Hated About Being a Woman

Reconciling Faith and Feminism

Christie Nafizger

Copyright © 2014 by Christie Nafziger
All rights reserved.
ISBN: 0692242074
ISBN-13: 978-0692242070 (10Things)
Library of Congress Control Number:
2014911626
10Things, Bradenton, Florida

Table of Contents

1. An Introduction — 1
   Origins of Dissent

2. Women Talk Too Much — 7
   MVP - Mars Venus Paradox

3. Women Are Emotional — 15
   The Emoto-tron

4. Women Are Nosy — 23
   Angle of Approach

5. Women Nag — 31
   Chalk Promises

6. Women Care How They Look — 39
   Robbed Blind

7. Women Want Romance — 45
   The Duet Diet

8. Women Care What People Think — 53
   Losing My Selfies

9. Women Are Targets — 61
   Beast Master

10. Women Cry   67
    Pour Me

11. Women Are Vulnerable   73
    Life After the Junkyard

12. Epilogue   83
    Reign Shelter

An Introduction
Origins of Dissent

This is a book about sex, not sexuality but a sex, women. I was born a woman. Maybe you can identify with that. Maybe you will identify with a lot of things I struggled with. This list of ten things won't shock you. You may not see yourself as a hater of these. They will most likely sound "stereotypical" to you.
Stereotypes are funny things, aren't they? They are like a shoe that always seems to fit a little better than you'd like it to. Any which way it doesn't fit is most obvious to you, the person wearing it. I am not trying to sell you shoes. What I am telling you about is how badly I did not want these shoes to fit me. I did not want to walk in them, I did not want to try them on. I don't think I hated women, but I did not want to be one like "that." I was determined that shoe would not fit.

Sneak ahead if you want; check out the list, but the list is not the story, the list contains no healing. Maybe you have already assigned the role of the list. Is the list the enemy? Is the list the mantra of my enemy? Does the list define my enemy, the "me" worthy of derision and spite? Yes, all of the above at times, but that is not the end. When the Truth arrives in this story, in our story, it will reveal what is the lie and who the oppressor was all along. This sounds controversial right? More than you yet know.

I should warn you now, I have read the Bible and believe it. I know a lot has happened since the penning of its pages. Even within the brief history of this country the role of women in society has changed drastically. The Bible provides context to this change. How can you measure distance without a known origin? Without an origin we are only seeing variance inside a limited scope, un-oriented or disoriented.

Maybe you don't believe the Bible is the Word of God like I do. Maybe you believe the story it tells of Adam and Eve is a parable. Either way, to me this represents the origin for relationship between man and woman. I am going to assume a certain familiarity with this portion of scripture from Genesis. It has special meaning to me. It was as I read its passages that I got set free. I came to the line where Adam awoke and discovered her. His response surprised me. He said, "This is bone of my bone, and flesh of my flesh."[1] Beyond that he said if I am "ish", then this is "ishi." Not sure why that part mattered so much to me. I guess I heard it as "me" and "me too." I can honestly

---

[1] Genesis 2:23 (NIV).

Origins of Dissent

say I had never felt so accepted as a woman as I did at that moment. Then God said, "It is good." Loved, I knew I was loved and it started to change me, heal me, restore me as a man, a human, and as a woman.

So I have begun with the end. How I wish it were my beginning, but like you, I was not born at the origin. I got my start in an age with much distance from there, much history between men and women. It started with the fall and the blame game. It progressed through cycles of generational oppression and violence. I can't trace the history to draw the line, but I could feel it as I took my first breath as a woman unwanted. It wasn't my father's fault. He just wanted a son, an heir, someone more like him to carry his name. In most cultures today, female infants are not as highly valued. However, I have heard they are a prize, in small villages in Indonesia, where a daughter means you will never be poor. She will someday be old enough to be sent to the city and sold day after day in the sex industry.

But, here in America, I was born at a time of revolution, of war between the sexes. We were fighting for equality. Recent generations have made changes in that direction. They were pioneers, but did they know where we were going? When we started tearing down walls had we scouted the promised land? Any

10 Things I Hated About Being A Woman

woman born outside the garden could tell you something was wrong and I thank God for the women willing to fight to make it right. I had the privilege to come behind them and live in the freedom they had wrought for future generations of women. But it was not enough. I still felt second-class, like my body was made for a life of the lesser.

I loved and respected the men in my life, father, brother, uncles and grandfather. They encouraged me in sports and games usually reserved for boys in that day. It was when I grew out into the world I discovered what it meant to be a girl. There were limitations on my involvement in sport, expectations from other girls on my behavior, and uncomfortable overtures from boys I thought were my friends. I just wanted to be "one of the guys." I saw that movie. I saw all those movies: Tootsie, Yentl, The Journey of Natty Gann. I modeled my interactions after that pattern. I took on the demeanor, the look, the swagger of a young male. I put on the uniform thinking that if we were all one form they would see through me to me. But dressing up in this uniform did not make me any less a captive, because I still saw me through the eyes of "the other."

There is something about otherness. I believe it was part of the design. God had said, "It is not good for man to be alone." All that he

Origins of Dissent

made was good, but this, this loneness was not. The relationship between man and woman was not the only relationship kicked off in the garden. That was where man was made by his Creator and that relationship saw light of day. Maybe you are still hearing it as parable. That is ok, but hear it. I was mad at God. He made a mistake when he made me. I was sure I was supposed to be my brother. I was not supposed to be "the other." If only I could have seen my start. I was created by the Creator, an original. I was planned. I was sent here for such a time as this, a time of revolution, of war, of change, of restoration and reconciliation. I was born for it. You can call it destiny. I will call it His design. But, I . . . was born . . . a woman.

Women Talk Too Much
MVP - Mars Venus Paradox

Women talk too much. I bought this one, hook line and sinker. I am sorry to say that for a lot of years it shut me up. I didn't wanna be one of those women. I couldn't tell you where I first heard this and believed it. I think we've all heard it, through TV, men we know, men we don't know, other women maybe. But I took it to heart.

I can't say I was angry with myself every time I wanted to talk, but I was very conscious about talking too much. I would stop myself short, sometimes trailing off even before the end of a sentence or before I reached the end of a story. I was always in a hurry to get to the point just as quickly as I could. I am not sure if I devalued what I had to say in my own heart and mind. But I can tell you what I did do. I judged others. I judged other women. I agreed with the sentence pronounced upon them. I agreed that they talked too much. Anytime I heard a woman go on and on about something I would say, "She is one of those."

Can you see where I am going? How could I have been an abuser of women? How could I, who was born a woman misunderstand the design of a woman? How could I carry this vendetta against half the population?

In the "Men Are From Mars, Women Are From Venus" series, Dr. John Gray explains quite well the concept of female communication and thought.[2] He divulges what science has surmised. Often, a woman thinks while she speaks. Literally, she speaks to think. No wonder I thought I had nothing to say. I was short-circuiting the thought process. This can be difficult for males to understand, because they think before they speak . . . presumably. The effects of that could be totally irritating. You know what, that's totally forgivable. It is totally forgivable that a man would be frustrated by a woman who thinks differently than he does, who talks around the point until she gets there because she didn't know the point was where she was going. She has only just discovered it. It may be a valid point, even a profound point. He may not have seen it coming, regardless the trip was more than he had planned to endure. Some say this is just a theory. So keep the research coming then.

However, the missing component, that research cannot show you is how to forgive,

---

[2] John Gray, <u>Mars and Venus in the Workplace</u>, (NY, NY: HarperCollins Publishers, 2002) 32.

forgive someone for not being you, not thinking like you, not speaking like you, just not being YOU. The good thing, the glorious thing, is learning how to love another. It changes you. It makes you more than you were before. I believe that is why God said, "It is not good for man to be alone."[3] He knew that there was something more that he could be, that he could become.

    I recently got married. I have always been quiet, except for "that colic" as an infant. I had developed a very effective internal dialogue system for thinking. But I was also a good listener. In combo, that equaled shy. But something happened when I got married. I discovered what a wonderful soundboard my husband made. My internal dialogue went verbal. He jokes with me about how many words a day I need to get out, and he is glad I have friends to help meet my quotas. Call it the honeymoon phase if you want to, but he laments when I come home with nothing left to say.

    I am not saying that sometimes women aren't excessive in their communication, but they were born for it. It is part of our makeup. It's forgivable. It's understandable. It doesn't make us "less than." It doesn't make us stupid,

---

[3] **Genesis 2:18 (KJV).**

trivial, margin-able. Guess the amazing thing is that I can say "us" now, that I can accept that I talk like a woman. I think like a woman and I don't hate that. I get it. It makes me a better woman. Even writing this book, my thoughts are flowing as I pen the pages. In fact, I talked a lot of my notes into this. There is joy in it; there is liberty in it. There is no shame. There is no self-rejection. However, there is a form of rejection at work.

    I think communication is undervalued in our economy. In the U.S., we are not an agrarian society anymore and are increasingly less a manufacturing one. Maybe it is supply and demand, but networking, customer service, teaching, why do these skills come so cheap? For a long time, we have undervalued things which are "women's work" or that involve lots of talking. At least in these areas, we must entertain the idea that sometimes the best man for the job is a woman. Or else I am just an economical choice, a cheap knock-off for what could not be found. We should not be willing to accept that. I am not suggesting all women strive to excel in female dominated fields. I personally plowed a plot on the farm of mathematics. What I am saying is, we have artificially suppressed the value of certain skill sets. If we put our money where our mouth is and re-assessed the importance of how we treat people, we'd change more than the salary structure. "Whatever the market will bear" I suppose. Just be aware of what you bring to the negotiating table.

I have a friend who coaches competitive kids' soccer. He has coached winning boys' and girls' teams. He told me once that you coach girls differently than boys. He said some girls could be torn down like you would a boy. Yell at 'em when they mess up and they will get back up angry and ready to prove themselves. But other girls will be crushed. He said you just have to know your players. That sounds like good management to me. But I haven't met a lot of coaches or managers that can vary their strategy that way. I guess I am saying that I believe women are an untapped resource in business. We expect them to perform like men and be supported like men, while at the same time diminishing their innate skill set. I am not trying to demonize the system, just help the coach examine the bench.

On the other hand, the Bible has a lot to say about saying little. Ironic isn't it? Here is one Proverb: "Whoever guards his mouth and tongue keeps his soul from troubles."[4] Personally, I would rather hear chastisement from God in the privacy of His Word, than

---

[4] **Proverbs 21:23 (NKJV).**

from my boss publicly on any day. I think that was what Paul was talking about when he forbid women to talk in church, but rather to ask their husbands at home. If women talk to think, some of it could realistically be an internal dialogue, yes? The part of that scripture I have not heard applied to women is what he said next: "Or did the Word of God come originally from you? Or was it you only that it reached?"[5] Does this not imply God talks to women too? Look, if there was a competition for speaking time, I can understand why women had to bow out. It just wasn't a fair fight.

Maybe you can't hear it through the sarcasm, but I forgive Paul. I forgive the day in which he lived. Women didn't study the law the way men did back then. Perhaps, there was not time for it in that day. But we don't live in that day, do we? I am not giving precedence to circumstance, but "Study to show thyself approved"[6] can only apply to those given that opportunity. Can you see why women's education is so scary in parts of the world? It's the airtime, the communication space, as if there were only so many rooms in the Father's house. It is not so.

---

[5] 1 Corinthians 14:36 (NKJV).

[6] 2 Timothy 2:15 (KJV).

MVP - Mars Venus Paradox

It seems like a subtle difference, but it is an empowering one. Hold your tongue to give place to others or cut it off as character flaw? The question I'd pose to the Paul's of today: Is it better to encourage growth of the fruit of the Spirit, patience and self-control, or continue to say, "Sit down, shut up, you have nothing to say?" Maybe the former is how Paul meant it after all, but not how it has been portrayed for fear of saturation. Well it's time for maturation.

Ladies, that's us too. If we don't purposely hold our tongues sometimes, we might never listen, and everyone deserves a chance to be heard. "Let all things be done decently and in order."[7] "Let all things be done for the building up of the church."[8] Trust Him. He is a coach who knows His bench (or pew) and how to keep you AND your brothers motivated.

---

[7] 1 Corinthians 14:40 (NKJV).

[8] 1 Corinthians 14:26 (NIV).

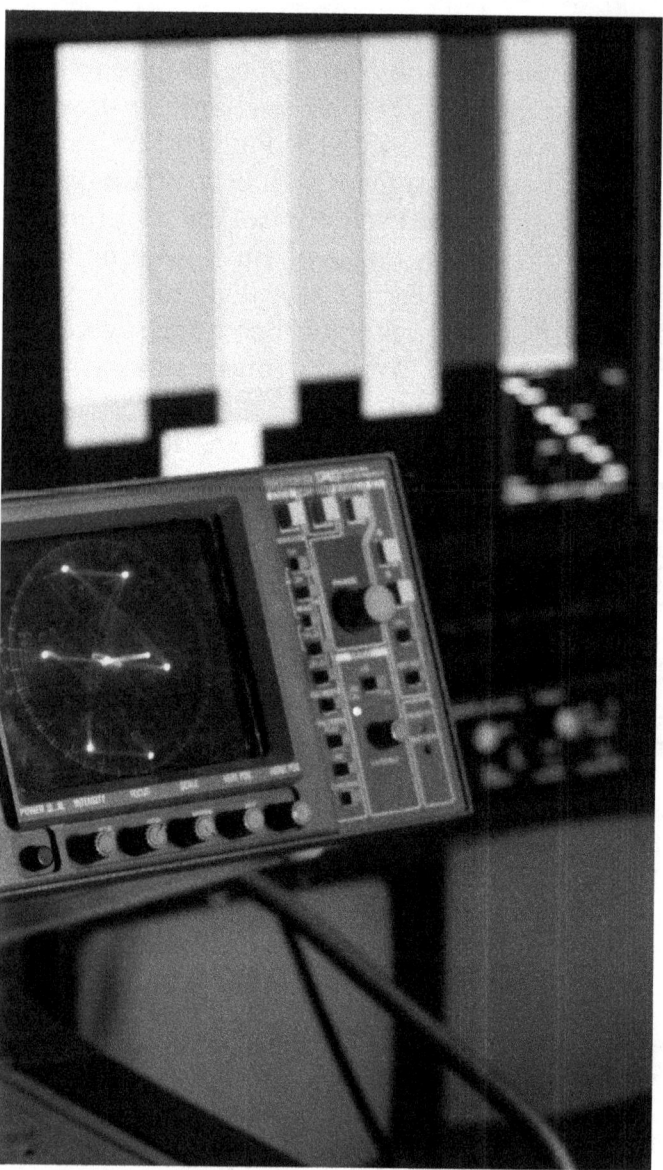

Women Are Emotional
The Emoto-tron

This topic takes us down, down deeper. Don't worry; it scares me a little too. It sounds sticky when you start talking about emotions. It is not something I'd wanna deal with. Maybe it is because I believed "women are too emotional." At the very least, I have misunderstood the role of emotions in being. If the emotional range is an instrument, a tool, it is NOT compass, but scope. Something like blips on a screen hitting or missing pre-outlined reference points. Scale and dimension determined by experience, real or imagined.

A friend of mine says, "You cannot follow your feelings because your feelings will always line up with your belief system. Your emotions will match even with lies you believe."[9] That is why we can't follow our feelings. But they become most useful when they reveal how well our beliefs are aligned with the truth. The truth compass is sold separately. The Bible, it says, "Buy the truth and do not sell it."[10] Pardon the jargon, but I

---

[9] Steve Lapp, Light of Hope Ministries, www.lightofhopeministries.com

[10] Proverbs 23:23 (NIV).

think it works like color bars. Color bars are a test pattern used in television and video to ensure a consistent signal. It helps identify loss or degradation. It registers on a vector-scope, each bar plotting points around an origin. In reality the appropriate range on the scope is set, but in our metaphor we choose what is normal. If we put the truth on our scope, we can see how it fits or doesn't. Any dissonance in a hue is cause for change, because the ultimate goal for our emotions is to rejoice with the truth.[11]

    I can't write this chapter as an overcomer. I still struggle here. But I don't hate myself for it. I am out of tune. I am often out of tune. But I am a sensitive instrument; my emotions are made to highlight truth and its beauty. But I miss the mark. I am sad at times without reason. I am ravaged by fear and worry needlessly. I wanna find peace in hope, but am unable because I don't believe. My faith is placed elsewhere, in more tragic outcomes. I want to show compassion, but am afraid of its cost.

    I have found a cheap substitute for proper calibration, an escape, a false scope: television. I can safely identify passively with characters that don't exist and situations which

---

[11] 1 Corinthians 13:6 (NIV).

The Emoto-tron

are contrived. My emotions can run wild here. My fears are almost always confirmed, predicted, and managed. I am right, but no closer to the truth. I have "loved" the lie. It is validating for me emotionally.

Understand that "calibration" is set from an outside source like color bars. What is your outside source? Maybe it is more like "whom." Who is your standard? Who sets the foundation for your beliefs? What is possible in your world, the high and low? What is likely? What do you fear? Fear becomes the black, the deepest darkest background, the base. It colors all the others. This almost sounds sinister, doesn't it? Likely, there is adjustment to be made. The standard according to the Word of God is fear of the Lord your God, "Let Him be your fear."[12]

What does this change? Selfishness, self-preservation. Who cares? About your life or anybody else's? Do I care? Am I capable of caring? I am afraid not. To care means to provide treatment or attend to someone or something. Am I capable of caring for someone other than me? As a woman, that matters to me. If I look deep, I find I was made to care, care deeply but cannot or will not. I'd say this is where I miss the mark most often.

---

[12] **Isaiah 8:13 (NKJV).**

10 Things I Hated About Being A Woman

I'd say this is what I am most emotional about. But why? Why do my emotions seem to keep pointing me back to this, this "love" thing? Why is "love" where my feelings go the most haywire?

I have been misled. Fear has led me here. It colored my path, highlighted what it wanted me to see. Fear made pretty the traps it'd laid out for me and made dark what might set me free. I have feared rejection. I have feared failure. I have feared abandonment. Can you see what I see? Places to hide, faces to avoid, gifts to bury in vaults of complacency? I have been robbed.

But occasionally, my black resets. I have seen the light in different hues. God is love and this sets anew my standard. How is that possible you say? If I fear Him, I fear what matters to Him. His preference, approval and disapproval become highlighted. My conscience resets the black and white. His joy gives color and vibrancy to an image we share. His laws and judgments are just and assign value to what is truly good. What does this mean for my emotions? Hope, emotions can't feel their way to love in the darkness, the darkness of my self-serving heart. His commands reveal how much He cares about how I treat others. That also means He cares as deeply about how others treat me. Together

The Emoto-tron

we see clearly how fear of abandonment and rejection oppresses and isolates. Together we conclude forgiveness of human weakness is in order. Together we celebrate the strength it takes to be the first to try, the first to love. Seeing things His way changes the dismal grey that saturated my eyes with fear of lesser things. Who is your standard? Who is your truth?

In the day-to-day battle, are you alone? It is fruitless to discuss strategy for war but walk around unarmed. Emotions follow belief, but belief can be led by thoughts. "As a man thinks in his heart, so is he."[13] A thought forms a line in your scope, a wrinkle, a trough to fall into. But not every thought conforms to the truth. The good news is that you don't have to follow every thought. The Bible talks about taking your thoughts captive and bringing them into the obedience of Christ. You are not alone you have an ally, who models truth in every situation, who makes the way straight.

Say your heart is burdened, sadness prevails, mourning lingers longer than her due. We "don't mourn as those who have no hope."[14] What is it you are thinking? What is the thought pattern that is oppressing you?

---

[13] **Proverbs 23:7 (NKJV).**

[14] **1 Thessalonians 4:13 (NLT).**

10 Things I Hated About Being A Woman

What is the fear? What is the lie? If you are out of tune with the truth, there is something to be confronted by His banner and your emotional scope. It comes to the surface to be dealt with. But He is also Comforter and Counselor who collects our tears in a bottle. He hears our cries, gives ear to our grievances. Perhaps, that is the truth we have not believed, that we are heard, known and loved.

Perhaps, in the absence of a just hearer, we have become angry taking on the labor of revenge, replaying injuries inside an empty box where the pain can only reverberate off cold walls, serving to perpetuate feelings of anger. Thinking yourself the one, true, righteous judge brings no peace. We need to have our grievances heard, if not by the king at least by the prince . . . the Prince of Peace.

We need to know that God is a just God, that He cares about how others treat us and what happens to us if we are to trust His standard. But look what He allowed to happen to His own son. How can we trust a God like that? This, this cross, is where we see forgiveness was not free, but it has been paid for. Not just for me, but for my enemies as well. This is where we know our cries have been heard. He knows this is what they deserve and where justice has been served. He is making peace by being broken. Mourn for

The Emoto-tron

Him and forgive. Jesus said, "Father forgive them, for they do not know what they do."[15] So don't cry for them, cry for Jesus. Set this as the origin for your scope, the center, the beginning and end of the color spectrum.

"Weeping may endure for a night, but joy cometh in the morning."[16] Joy is what we are all aiming for, right? There is nothing more attractive on a woman than joy. It is what we are made for. You can try and fake it, tune yourself through deception to react to lesser stimuli. This is what you were made for, to resonate with the Truth . . . deeply, passionately, with all of your heart, your soul, and your strength. Rejoicing is not just about joy. It is also about strength. It is in this light that I encourage us with these words: Recalibrate and rejoice for His banner, His standard over us is LOVE!

---

[15] Luke 23:34 (NKJV).

[16] Psalm 30:5 (KJV).

Women Are Nosy
Angle of Approach

If it weren't for nosy people, I wouldn't "knows" anybody. I am a bit of an introvert. I speak when I have something to say and try to mind my own business. If everyone were like me, the world would be a quiet, boring place. So I kind of like nosy people, the kind that ask you how you are doing, and listen for an answer. There are people who remember your name and the name of your family members. I have always wondered why, why they care at all.

Ya know, the Bible talks about busybodies, people with idle hands, meddling in the affairs of others. But it also talks about compassion and bearing one another's burdens. It even says, "A man who has friends must himself be friendly."[17] I have been working toward being this kind of person, this kind of "nosy." It's not that I don't have enough friends or you don't have enough already. It's that love grows everywhere you go . . . or it doesn't. I am finally feeling like I have something to share, something to give, and it pleases my heavenly Father.

---

[17] Proverbs 18:24 (NKJV).

10 Things I Hated About Being A Woman

Grandma used to say that Grandpa never met a stranger. He was always chatting with the waiter or waitress, joking and laughing. He talked to strangers in the TV department where patient husbands waited for their wives to finish shopping. We'd come to find him and he'd made a new friend every time. I know they may not have had deep, meaningful conversation, but it made the moment better, memorable maybe. What if life could be more like that? Instead of following a path leading only from task to task, we could walk that same road from person to person, conversation to conversation?

I am not saying avoid work, talk yourself out of a job, or do nothing but approach others randomly. Don't have idle hands. Mind your business, but mind God's too. He's in the people business. As you go about your labor, you will run into a few people. They are common in commerce. Transactions may someday all be done by computer, but today there is opportunity to make eye contact with a human being, to smile, to say thank you and mean it. They have a name and maybe a second name, a family name. Therefore, they likely have a family.

I don't know where you are going, how much time you have, the pace you set yourself. I know my day goes by too quickly and faces

Angle of Approach

blur if I ever see them at all. What if in all my doing, I have left the really valuable part undone, like forgotten bags in the checkout line. What if God is not pleased with how quickly I ran the race, because I took short cuts around all the obstacles? What if God's plan wasn't for us to treat other people like obstacles in our path? What if . . . what if they were the path?

There was a time in this country when people lived farther apart. When you went into town, you knew you would see people, talk to people because that was different than being at home with you and yours. Going to town was a social outing as well as a goods gathering or wares selling trip. Hearing stories, catching up, and meeting people was "par for the course." I understand there were "sand traps" like gossip and rumor, but don't get hung up there. Stick to the "fairways." Church, for example, was an all-day event. You gathered, worshipped, heard a sermon, had a meal, visited with people you had not seen all week, and headed home just before sunset. Now that was an event worth "teeing up" for.

Maybe it should be easier today with our motor driven buggies, but it's not. Personally, I have a hard time just getting out there in the game. I think what I most fear are the "water hazards." How do I respond to those who mourn, whose tears have puddled up before me? I understand comforting with the same comfort wherewith you are comforted or mourning with those who mourn. But how do I find *"my ball"* again? I mean it is so easy to get caught up in another's sorrow and carry it home with you. How do you keep from taking a bucket full for your own? I am guessing the answer has something to do with prayer. If you find yourself burdened for another, intercession seems a proper response. But it can be hard to separate your emotions sometimes as a woman. You forget why you are feeling this way. You forget that it is not your own tear "pond."

Imagination is powerful. It powers our compassion. If you think about it, we are imagining how the other person feels or is affected by events that actually did not happen to us. Jesus moved toward the crowd with compassion and healed them. Of course, given who He was, "If you've done it unto the least of these you have done it unto Me," could mean He was more present than imagined. [18] But for us, we do a lot of imagining and parts of our brain can't tell the difference. That is

---

[18] **Matthew 25:40 (NIV).**

Angle of Approach

why we cry at a sad movie, or jump at a scary one.

Do you ever move toward your TV screen with compassion? I hope not. But if not, what might that mean to our ability to move in compassion? Are we subtly training ourselves to harvest passivity when it comes to envisioning others emotions? Are we honing our emotional IQ while training complacency? And what happens if you take home a bucket of fictional sorrow? Can you give that to God or does it just become a part of your own landscape, shaping the curbside appeal of your worldview? We watch so much tragedy on TV that God can't do anything about because it isn't real. Then when life even reminds us of something we saw on TV, it validates the 100 programs that portrayed similar circumstance. Can you tell your mind that it only happened once or will all associated memories rise to counter? I am not saying TV is evil. I am saying what we all already know: it is not real.

The people you see everyday are. I think part of why their story holds so little interest for us is because we have grown fat on stories. We don't need to hear about a stranger's life. We have friends on speed dial that will meet us on our timetable in front of the couch. They won't judge us or care how we judge them. They open up their lives to us

10 Things I Hated About Being A Woman

without question. Sure, maybe they are trying to sell something, but we are in control, we are the consumers right? Yes, but is that all we are? Is that the only goal of commerce? It doesn't have to be. There is a you and me on either side of every transaction, sale or purchase. The work you do to earn a dollar, you don't do alone, do ya? You've got co-workers? Who is your neighbor? Maybe it isn't just the person next door, maybe it's the person you just held the door for on your way to market. Maybe "par for this course" isn't good enough. What kind of game are we playing here? Dodging the "obstacles" and "playing through" are part of a past-time where less is better, lower is greater. Who is counting your swings, tallying your "strokes?" Are you so certain of the "flag" you targeted? Take an extra swing or two, step out of the fast lane, try it. Be nosy for Heaven's sake. I will, if you will. What have you got to lose?

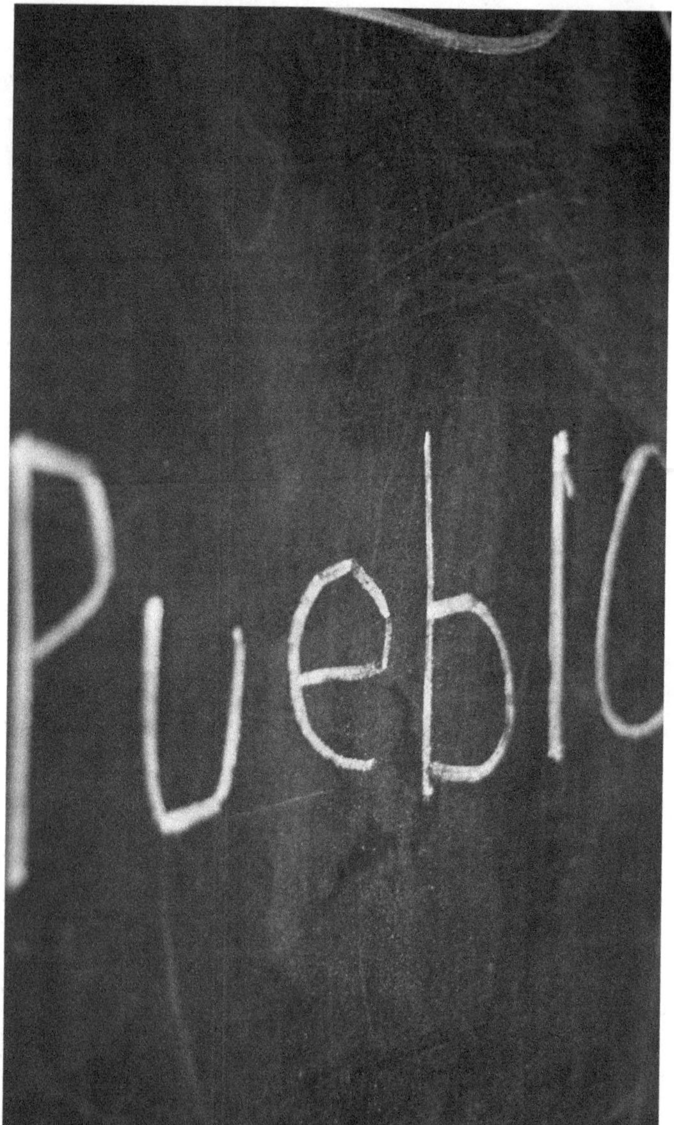
Pueblo

Women Nag
Chalk Promises

The bible talks about a contentious and angry woman being like a continual dripping. Some translations say "nagging" there. Ani DiFranco, a folk singer whose philosophy I once subscribed to, wrote that "every tool is a weapon if you hold it right."[19] That's what I think of when we talk about nagging, a tool turned weapon. But to put it another way, from the perspective of Myles Munroe, "If the purpose of a thing is misunderstood, abuse is inevitable."[20] He was speaking about how some men treat women when he preached that. If a man doesn't know what a woman is good for, what she is made for, then he may end up abusing her or misusing her. On the other hand, a woman, if she doesn't know how to put her gift of gab to good could wound somebody with water torture.

God designed woman to be a helpmate. What kind of helpmate would she be if she did not offer an alarm, a reminder, like your

---

[19] Ani DiFranco, "IQ," <u>Puddle Dive</u> (Buffalo, NY: RighteousBabe Records, 1993).

[20] Myles Munroe, Bahamas Faith Ministries International Fellowship, www.bfmmm.com

phone? I heard a joke once that went: "How do you stop a woman from nagging?" The answer: "Do it the first time she asks." But seriously, I don't believe that is the answer. The best answer is a biblical one. The Bible urges us to "let your yes be yes and your no be no."[21] Meaning, if you don't plan on doing something, don't say that you will. Granted it may be a confrontation right out of the box, but at least you won't keep draggin' the naggin'. You know the rest of that verse goes, "Let your yes be yes and your no be no; anything beyond this comes from the evil one."[22] I am not pointing fingers here. I am just saying that it might be better not to make excuses or pretend.

    I am not a particularly good nagger. I think that is why I didn't make a great teacher. "Your homework is on the board. . . . Remember to do your homework. . . . Did you do your homework? . . . Where is your homework? . . . Turn in your homework. . . . Did you study for your test?" It is a skill, let me tell you. It requires patience, endurance, and tenacity.

    The dictionary definition of excuse is a plea offered in extenuation of a fault or for release from an obligation or promise. A friend

---

[21] James 5:12 (NKJV).

[22] Matthew 5:37 (NIV).

Chalk Promises

of mine calls an excuse "a well planned lie."[23] I suppose if you include a broken promise as a lie, then it fits. Trust is extremely important to a woman. It is the cornerstone of intimacy, even intimacy with our Creator. In His word, He made a lot of promises. Then He says, "Ask and it shall be given."[24] Jesus tells the story of the woman and the unjust judge.[25] She pleaded repetitiously for justice. In the end, he gave her what she sought not for fear of God, but so she would cease requesting. A woman will fight for a cause until she feels it has been given a fair hearing. Hmm. I wonder if there is an appeals process? I suppose it depends in part on whether you believe the judge is just in his hearing.

On the other hand, I suppose in business this tenacity may have economic value. There is a market for the ability to knock and keep knocking until the door is opened. The thought is scary when it's telemarketers, but inspiring when it's an industrious startup seeking capital. Ya know it's not rejection that increases this drive. It's

---

[23] Steve Lapp, Light of Hope Ministries, www.lightofhopeministries.com

[24] Matthew 7:7 (KJV).

[25] Luke 18.

the occasional "yes" that gives hope. So you can train for nagging by occasionally giving in. Good to know? Let your "yes be yes and ..."

No. There are some people who can't hear "no." There are also some people who can't say "no." The two make quite a pair when they get together as you can imagine. I read this in a book on Boundaries.[26] I'd suppose I land closer to the "can't-say-no" camp. But, I am aware of it and God's direction "No be no," helps support my resolve. To get out of saying "no" I have taken on things I should not rather than break a promise. It produces a sort of resentment and avoidance in places I try not to reveal. It even makes it hard for me to ask for favors since I assume most people will also have trouble answering honestly. If you can't say no, then what is your true motivation? Obligation? Not the most joyful labor of love. I suppose you can trust it if you get a yes. But, what if someone like me gets a no. How do we interpret that? Well from our own experience we may judge someone. We may assume they are less committed than we are or are more selfish. I am not condoning this thought process, just revealing it, confessing it.

---

[26] Dr. Henry Cloud, and Dr. John Townsend, <u>Boundaries</u>, (Grand Rapids, MI: Zondervan, 1992) 61. <u>www.BoundariesBooks.com</u>

Chalk Promises

I'd say your best naggers would land closer to the "can't-hear-no" camp. The book I reference here gives a clear list of experiences/disappointments that could lead someone to be unable to receive a negative answer.[27] I think it presupposes an unjust judge. This could of course initiate the appeals process. A yes at that point would be motivated by annoyance. This also is no labor of love. If love is what the petitioner was seeking, a yes so wrought will feel a somewhat hollow victory, albeit a familiar one. Would you agree sometimes it may be better to trust the judge for an honest answer, an earnest reply? This alone allows the space needed for love to be the motivation. Not obligation. Not irritation. Love.

Ultimately, I guess I'd say there is a purpose for nagging under heaven, a season for it. There is a time to nag and a time to refrain from nagging. I visited the Pueblo cliff dwellings near the four corners region once. Our guide described the diapers the Anasazi had used. He said they were made from juniper bark. He imagined how excellent they were for potty training. A child only had to ask, "What do I need to do to get out of these things again?" I am not advocating irritating, juniper diapers for grown men (unless that is

---

[27] Cloud & Townsend, 63-84.

10 Things I Hated About Being A Woman

the kind of relationship you are looking for). I am saying, I hope this is something we can all grow out of.

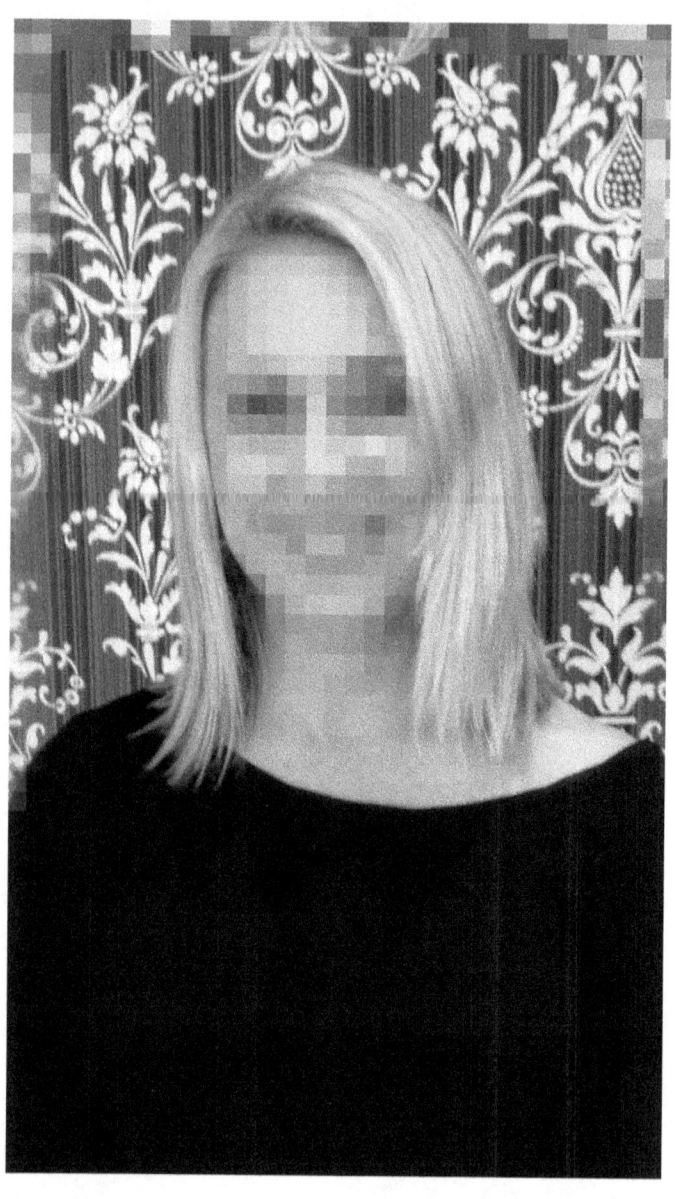

Women Care How They Look
Robbed Blind

"Beauty is in the eye of the beholder." How do you look? How you read that question says a lot in light of the statement that precedes it. Maybe you saw yourself in the mirror last or you have a clear concept in your mind of what you think you "look like." But odds are you aren't standing in the mirror right now. Maybe you are reading words on a page. Stop. Look up. What do you see all around you? You are not the object. You're the beholder. Look. How do YOU look? What do YOU see? What do YOU admire, esteem, hold as valuable? Who do you admire and what is associated with that admiration? Is that what or who you want to "look like?" You are being conformed to the world by what you see and how you weigh its worth. Why do you continue to hand yourself back to the world and ask it to weigh you? We care so much about what other's are looking at, that we don't know how we "look?"

A friend of mine is a hair stylist. She says most of the times when people bring in a picture to illustrate the cut they want, it is a picture of a celebrity, of course. Makes sense since they have high-end stylists at their beck and call. But she knows her clients and will often ask what it is they like about the cut. Sometimes it is effective to cover the face of the celebrity so only the hair is visible and ask the same question. It allows the hair to speak for itself and not all the associations attached to the star. She finds it often communicates something else, that can help the client get the cut they really want.

So I'll ask again. Who do you admire and why? Pretend for a second it's not the clothes or the hair, because those have all found value attached to something or someone else. What is valuable in your eyes? Look, really look. Dust off your scales, the scales that weigh things. Not all that glitters is gold. Test it. Put something you know the value of on one side . . . honesty, integrity, kindness, goodness, love. Now compare. What do you esteem, prize, or praise? Our praise has been given away so easily. We have been clapping along so long, we don't set the standard, we don't raise it or appraise it. We just measure ourselves by it.

Maybe you don't wanna be the judge. The Bible says, "That by the same measure with which you judge, you shall be judged."[28] Is that why we abdicate the throne? Who am I that I should say who is good? Well, I am not

---

[28] **Matthew 7:2 (NIV).**

talking about judging other people. I am talking about "be not afraid of their faces."[29] What do you like about that haircut? What do you like about what this person does or says? How do you look at others? What are you seeing that is worth something more than nothing? These value assignments will become the tools of measurement for you too. What is the effect of what you saw, the fruit that sight bears in your own life? What or who are you looking like? You have conformed to a standard, but whose if not your own?

Here is a word we have misdefined, "vanity." We think somehow it is defined as self-seeking, but Biblically it means failure, pointless, worthless, bearing no fruit or good. We see it repeatedly as men and women try in vain to ... "x, y, z." You should read a couple scriptures for yourself. I cannot bear the chastisement and conviction here. I will convey one: "Let us not be desirous of vain glory, provoking one another, envying one another."[30] What sort of glory is vain, is hollow, is worthless? Don't ask me. Don't ask the kings and queens of the "silver screen," a schoolmate, or anyone trying to sell you something. I don't see what you see and

---

[29] Jeremiah 1:8 (KJV).

[30] Galatians 5:26 (KJV).

neither do they. You are the judge in this beauty contest. The contestants aren't people, but ideas, principles, visions of beauty that shape your own beauty, frame it and reveal it. Hey, I will admit that my scale was broken and every measure a lie. If we can, for a moment, humble ourselves and ask the Manufacturer. He wrote a manual and has an 800 #. He reset my weights and measures for free.

Listen, you know you are gonna take cues from a throne, look up to some royalty somewhere. Why not the Most High, because everything else is worth a little less? "Shall He who formed the eye not see?[31] Before I said, "I don't see what you see." Well He does. He isn't going to interrupt your programming to tell you what He wants you to see ... unless you ask Him to. Every time we do, He fine-tunes our perception and our reception. At last, you can look in the mirror and see what He sees. He is the only One who will truly see you, because He sees what you have seen. He sees you from the inside looking out. He beholds the beholder.

He says, "If the eye be full of light, than the whole body is full of light."[32] Maybe we don't care enough about how we "look."

---

[31] **Psalm 94:9 (KJV).**

[32] **Matthew 6:22 (NKJV).**

Robbed Blind

Maybe if we did we'd be more empowered, not less. The Lord of all the Earth is seeking such as these. He says in His Song of Songs: "Who is she who looks forth as the morning, Fair as the moon Clear as the sun, Awesome as an army with banners?"[33]

---

[33] Song of Solomon 6:10 (NKJV).

Women Want Romance
The Duet Diet

What has limited love? How did love get so hemmed in? Who has reduced it to a box of chocolates? Chocolates taste good, feel good, and last only for a moment. The box itself sets boundaries, protects, conceals, orders, and confines. Maybe you think I am talking about marriage, but I am not. I am talking about where your heart is shared, where you are willing to love and be loved. This is gonna sound strange at first because we have been brainwashed, but love wasn't meant to be shared by just two people.

"Wait what?!? I thought you were Christian."

Yeah and Jesus said love your neighbor as yourself.

"Gross."

You see we have taken the limits off our sexual self-restraint and reduced our vows to good intentions. While at the same time, we cut ourselves off from investing in relationships we can't get our teeth into. Sounds like the zombie apocalypse to me, consuming each other upon our lusts. Guess that could happen when the food supply is strategically limited. We were made for love; we hunger for it and starve without it. We

10 Things I Hated About Being A Woman

have put ourselves on a strict diet, a diet in which love is only available in the context of a sexual relationship, "eros love." We even limit our use of that word, saying that word is used too much. Even the word gets withheld, until achieving a certain level in a sexual relationship. We are so famished by that point we will melt at the thought of being told we are loved. This is a fact easily exploited by some men. A simple "I love you" and she will do anything. It's like rain in the desert, but is life meant to be so dry?

    Open up your narrow definition of love, kick the top off the box. There are rivers flowing here. Let me give you a handful of them. Have you heard of the five love languages?[34] Great couples' therapy book, but also a great road map for unmarked wells. The languages are: quality time, words of affirmation, acts of service, gifts, and touch. Purposely left touch last since you are having such a hard time separating sex and love, but it is still in there for when you grow up.

    Quality time is expensive. No wonder you are so picky about who you give that to.

---

[34] Gary Chapman, <u>The 5 Love Languages: The Secret of Love That Lasts</u>, (Chicago, IL: Northfield Publishing, 1992). www.5lovelanguages.com

The Duet Diet

But, do you give it away sometimes to family or friends? Admit this is love. Spending time together is showing love, giving and receiving it. This is one of my primary love languages and I am stingy with it I admit. Many marital relationships suffer from suffocation. People spend less time with friends or family and make their spouse wholly accountable to meet their quality time needs. Wonder why we are so desperate for "romance?"

Words of affirmation can be cheap, but if you fake it you will only assume everyone else does too. Let your yes be yes. If you ain't got nothing nice to say, don't say anything. But love speaks. Look for opportunities to genuinely encourage somebody. Why are you stingy with that? It doesn't cost anything, but the change in your perspective. Instead of tearing others down all around you, try lifting them up. Will you feel more loved by doing that for others? Maybe not, but maybe so. If you only knew the pleasure of your heavenly Father in this endeavor, His joy would be your strength. Did you know He told Peter three times, "If you love me, feed my sheep?"

Acts of service were my grandma's number one love language, at least on the giving side. I did not understand that growing up. I felt loved, but I thought she was a slave to it. Never once did I imagine her sacrifice as an act of love, every meal, every car ride, every clean towel. She took us in and loved us. Sorry to say I took that for granted at the time, focusing more on the havoc in my young life. I see things differently now. I am more thankful when someone does something for me. It doesn't go unnoticed or unacknowledged. I am a better tipper for it. I know they do it for money, but I receive it with love. Why reduce it to transaction? Guess I am trying to make it too easy for you by keeping it close to home. Maybe you need to get out, get out and volunteer for something, for someone. Jesus said, "Whoever desires to be great among you shall be your servant."[35] Will you feel more loved? Yes, because you will recognize its value, you will have counted the cost when you receive love in this form.

    Thinking about cost, let us discuss gifts. Ever hear, "It's the thought that counts?" Well it does. The thought comes before the gift. A gift doesn't just set itself in motion. It is born of a thought. I guess it is sort of a manifestation of a thought, of good will, strong will even since you have to will yourself out of your comfort to procure it and deliver it. This is obviously not my primary love language, but lots of women love to shop. Part of that is shopping

---

[35] Mark 10:43 (NKJV).

The Duet Diet

for others, or can be. It starts with the thought of another, their need, their desire, and the hope of their joy. It culminates, I am told, with the "presentation." A gift should be worthy of the thought start to finish. A gift should look like a gift and that's all in the presentation. We get wrapped up in our own lives by our selfish nature. Being a thought on another's heart is a win for love, but so is having the thought of another's heart. Hey, they have a heart! Let that unfold.

Finally, let's touch on touch. Guess this is as good a place as any to tell you. You were born through sex. Two very specific parts of the body touched and dot, dot, dot you were born. That . . . is not an empty space. We pretend it is, but it isn't. I think we have believed that sex made us, that we were born of the will of sex, and formed for its pleasure. Well that's what you come up with when you take God out of the uterus: "sex slaves." In scripture it says, "You knit me together in my mother's womb."[36] God made you, you were born of His will, and formed for His pleasure. If God is Love, than Love made you, you were born of Love, and formed for Love.

Still can't separate it yet? That's because we don't know love like that. But it is there. It

---

[36] **Psalm 139:13 (NIV).**

is in the marrow of our bones. Our love bones have been formed lacking nutrients. We have grown them strong on vitamins T.V. and XXX. The meaning of love has been calcified in our virtual experience. In a purely visual world, love looks like touch. How else can you SEE it? Used to just be the kiss, but that's not enough now. If you only have an hour to convey love, show it, teach it, how would you do it, a box of chocolates maybe? That'll sell until the bones rot.

But the grave is not the only solution. There is a sword capable of separating the joints and the marrow, dividing the SEX=LOVE equation we have taken as postulate. That logic-defying sword is the very Word of God. Discover it and rediscover what LOVE is. Love is to be grandly applied to life. You were made for Love. Isn't that romantic?

Hug somebody. Hold the hand of a sick friend. Kiss your kids good night after you thank the One that made you both. If you know His love, than you know nothing can touch that. "His love never fails."[37] Let Him define Love for you, it's who He is.

---

[37] 1 Corinthians 13:8 (NIV).

Women Care What People Think
Losing My Selfies

What do others think or feel? Are others real? I think women have a keen awareness of the possibility that other people may have thoughts and feelings similar to their own. They may at least have some capacity to function as an independent being with faculties not unlike mine, yet not mine. It can lead them to ask, "If it is the case that this is a "person" as I am a "person," how should I respond to them?"

My husband is often frustrated by this tendency in me. I see someone in a hurry to get around me in the supermarket and move out of the way. "Why?" he wonders. I suppose it is because if it were my need I would want someone to move. It is what I would want in their situation. He has warned me that this behavior and way of thinking could paralyze me with indecision. He has a point.

However, this "compassion" is not a part of me that I am okay with severing from my being. So, I am deciding I need a plan of attack. I need to know how I am supposed to respond to the needs, attitudes, and discomfort of others before it comes up. It is an adventure,

10 Things I Hated About Being A Woman

this exploring of "love your neighbor as yourself" and what that means, like a safari. I don't have all the answers so I wait for them, watch for them. What I really need to find is a role model, someone to show me how to treat other people. I call this search a hunt, as it is not a full-service dining experience, because you cannot passively accept what is served to you. It is not a witch-hunt. I am not seeking power over anyone or to condemn character flaws. Rather, I am a marksman, seeking the mark of "beauty." A beauty mark not on the outside, but a "hallmark" of the kind of beauty you can walk in from door to door and face to face. True beauty can't be captured from the flicker of self-reflection. How can I see compassionately when I am solely concerned about what others are thinking about me? I want to train my eyes to see through the smoke and mirrors to catch a glimpse of real kindness, genuine generosity, and sacrificial love. I want to catch it, bottle it in memory, and one day wear it like Grandmother's perfume.

      Perhaps, I smell like a coward as I look around. I find most people are more willing to fight to get their way than I am. I weigh the cost to me and am usually capable of affording it. I remember how others treat me matters to God, so I am not defenseless, even if I don't defend myself. How others treat me defines

Losing My Selfies

what manner of man they are in His eyes. Hard truth: if someone loves you, it really says more about them than it does about you. You really can't measure yourself by how others treat you, it is really quite the opposite. I have met women in the church that love without reason. They are kind to me and to others and I don't know why. I can't see what is in it for them. To me, their mystery is a great discovery. It opposes the reality of reality TV, where motives are always in question by design.

    That said, I have also discovered there are things worth fighting for. I have met and loved many a brawling woman. I am very comfortable with their "take charge" ways. Often those women have had to fight very hard for something in their lives, something worth fighting for. Both my mothers have been victims of spousal abuse, not at my father's hands (he is a gentle man). But they had to fight for survival and for their children's future. I think sometimes this can lead to a life of struggle. You learn to fight and never stop fighting, in part, because it works . . . most of the time. When it doesn't you fight harder, then it works . . . much of the time. It is like training really, for what I don't know, but the end result is a strong woman. You'd think men would respect "her" right? Some do, but they don't usually wanna work with one. Maybe it is because it accuses their manhood. Perhaps somewhere deep inside they know what made her a fighter and that points it's finger and says, "I will not be your victim. I will not be taken advantage of by you." I have been an angry woman, but rarely a vengeful one ... unless we are going to count self-deprecation, blaming myself and then taking it out on me. In that case, I have had my revenge time and again.

So maybe I am not the best one to describe the lines and what is worth withstanding. I am not the best role model. I have erred in a certain direction by choice or lack of courage. But I have also seen error in the other direction. There are so many variables, so many personalities and situations. Sometimes you stand up to a bully. Sometimes you turn the other cheek. Who knows what will yield the better fruit in the end? God knows. God knows how to redeem a bad situation, when, where, and how to stand. He gives wisdom by His Spirit of Holiness and through His Word. He gives boldness when it is needed. There are things I would not say or do but that He asks. It empowers me when I would not confront for myself. He comforts me when others mistreat me because it matters to Him. But then, when it is time to repent for

Losing My Selfies

how I have treated others, He is quick to convict and forgive. So He grows me and approves me as the weaker vessel, ready for His use in any situation.

Do I care what others think? Yes, but they are in training too. I am part of their regimen, and they mine. We are all here learning how to love our neighbor as our self. But I am not helpful to them or they to me without the wisdom and perspective of God. He knows what I can bear, the weight I can't lift, the load I can't carry. His yoke is easy, His burden is light. The beginning of wisdom is the fear of God. In every exercise, I must fear Him more than the challenge or the challenger. With this carried in my mind's eye, I am free to grow and love others as they grow. The result will be the kind of strength God can find joy in.

You can see that I am not you. I will never become you. I am me. I exist. I am aware of my being, conscious of it, a separate individual with thoughts of my own to conceal or share. I was created by the Great "I AM" to live in the world He created to share with other "I am's." Apparently, He has some ideas about how to live in such a world. So I seek Him in it, hunt for the image of Him, the mark of beauty He has shared with His creation. If I have any lingering doubts about how He thinks we are to participate in existence, He sent His only son to be the ultimate role model. Jesus said, "If you had known Me, you would have known My Father also."[38] Herein is our love made complete . . . that as He is, so are we in this world.[39] My life is a gift, the gift of life is given to a "me," an "I am," an individual, one. From here, "I" can relate and be in relation to all the "I ams" of creation, including the Great I Am. The question I may ponder eternally is "Why would He die for ME?" Pursuing that answer changes my everything.

---

[38] John 14:7 (NKJV).

[39] 1 John 4:17 (NKJV).

Women Are Targets
Beast Master

Zombie movies hold interest for me because they make light of my plight. Somewhere, sometime in my development, I began to feel like there was a segment of the population that viewed me as a piece of meat. It was eager to help me to identify as either human leg or breast, white or dark. Recently, I have gone up a couple sizes. It is unacceptable, I know. Better to carve a little off the bone, maybe that would be easier to swallow. Television and magazines encourage me to separate off my best parts for marketing purposes. As if somehow I could be dissected, then sold to a "meat market." The message that we are bred to consume, spins around on me the "consumer" showing me my value as commodity, consumable. It is eat and be eaten at the bottom of the flesh chain. Welcome to womanhood.

But we can't go around blaming men for the images we are bombarded with anymore than Adam should have blamed Eve. "Look, it's pleasant to the eyes and tasty to eat," they say.[40] Didn't we learn anything from the fall, that it was within his authority to say, "No!

---

[40] Genesis 3:6 (KJV).

10 Things I Hated About Being A Woman

God says, 'No.'" Peer pressure is no excuse. You wouldn't accept that from your son or daughter. According to Jesus, even looking upon a woman to lust after her, you have already committed adultery with her in your heart.[41] "Did God really say that?"[42] Heard that question somewhere before. It is what the enemy said to Eve to talk her into crossing God. Talk about your meat cleaver, in marriage, a man is supposed to leave his mother and father and cleave unto his wife.[43] This tells me God knows how hard it is for men. He has always known

    In the garden of Eden, God brought every living creature to Adam to see what he would call them.[44] Quite an honor to give names to what you had not created. But there was not found among the beasts of the field or the birds of the air a companion suitable for him. So God created woman. She was meet for him, not meat for his belly. They were both

---

[41] Matthew 5:28 (NKJV).

[42] Genesis 3:1 (NKJV).

[43] Genesis 2:24 (KJV).

[44] Genesis 2:19 (KJV).

naked and not ashamed.[45] He had met his match and gave her his name. Together, they were "man," one flesh.

It is easy to see how confusing things can be, if we think we are all animals. Women become targets, something at which to take aim. Even if you hit it, you may not take it home for nourishment or display. It was just about firing your shot, target practice to improve your aim, prove and improve a skill. It is a game I'd rather not play from either side, but definitely not as the "prey." I suppose in an attempt to alter the roles, women buy into "sexy." Sexy is a power word and women know it. We lord it over men like it is a strength. We draw them in and then laugh as they draw their swords. But in reality, we only make the game more challenging and perpetuate tyranny by seeking its throne. Sexy is a wrestling match waiting to happen. So let it wait. Let it wait until marriage, where there are no winners or losers. Every match is a win-win, and a rematch is already scheduled.

I look at pictures of my grandmother from her youth. She was very beautiful. You can still see it if you look at her. It is in her smile, her laugh, her eyes. The beauty lingers. On the other hand, "sexy" burns like a hot

---

[45] **Genesis 2:25 (NKJV).**

10 Things I Hated About Being A Woman

flame and then its power is exhausted, like fireworks. Woe to a relationship fueled by sexy, it will soon be in energy crisis, searching for alternative resources. Hopefully these can be found at home and not abroad, on foreign shores. This fear paints other women as adversaries, further increasing isolationism.

Under this foreign policy, my zombie nightmare crescendos. I compete for resources, distrustful of other women and am chased by men, hungry for power over me. Shall I find refuge in a prison cell? Yes, I exaggerate, but you must see the parallels. This is not the world I want to live in. But this is a home built on the foundation sex=love. They are not interchangeable. "Our bodies were made for love." Is that the same as "Our bodies were made for sex?" Zombie apocalypse awaits.

Compare this with the Garden of Eden. It wasn't until after the fall that Adam named her "Eve," mother of all living. What if this means more than we think about male and female relations? Don't call me a heretic, but what if that means all men are to treat women like mothers, until the day they leave mother and father and are joined unto their wives. I am just saying, what if. What if when Jesus told Peter from the cross, Son behold your mother, and mother behold your son, He was doing more than tying up loose ends? Blessed

Beast Master

is Mary among women, but she is among women.

I have been reading about "chivalry." That'd make a good book for a man to write. Might help our soldiers returning from war to remember who they are in peace. One of the origins of the word was horseman. The code declared how a man was to treat a lady, the honor and esteem he was to bestow on her kind. The code encompassed much more than this about good deeds, defending the defenseless, and bravery. Women wait for a knight in shining armor and our King, our true King, is returning as a horseman riding a white horse. Makes me wonder what skills a young man needs to become adept in. Gathering numbers, notching headboards seem such vanity in the face of the real enemy.

I wish I could take the air out of this one, and say I am not angry anymore. But I am. The anger has changed some. I am not fighting from the perspective of a victimized target. I am a disappointed "mother." We can do better than this. I don't look at all men as possible mates. I see sons. I see sons of God, who I would gladly cheer in battle if someone would but train them.

Women Cry
Pour Me

Women cry. Men cry. Jesus cried, King David cried, a lot. People wept, and not just at funerals. God's people cried out in their slavery and He heard them from heaven. Most of David's weeping was done in private with God, but someone saw and David himself unabashedly wrote about it. It was part of experiencing trial and travail. The most important thing is God heard. He collects tears in a bottle.[46] He comforts the broken. Crying is part of God experiencing life with us. So why it is only socially acceptable at funerals?

I think part of why crying has become so unacceptable is because of our sense of responsibility. Crying is part of processing some strong emotions. So then why do we feel responsible when someone else cries? Don't know what to do? Let them process. Personally, I prefer to process in private, but when you've got something to say right away you can't always duck into a prayer closet. I have had to deliver some pretty honest speeches through tears, because it was now or never. Not sure of the consequences on my reputation, but my second option was a quick

---

[46] Psalm 56:8 (NKJV).

10 Things I Hated About Being A Woman

exit. Personally, I think it took more guts to stand and deliver through tears.

When I first got reconnected to God, I'd be standing there in a worship service singing, or not, and tears would start streaming down my face. I would try to wipe them away before anyone could see and get a little frustrated with God for embarrassing me. Of course, I always felt better if I just closed my eyes and let the tears roll. I remember a woman who was weeping at the altar. She got up and said, "I have been dry too long." I never really understood what she meant.

I am young. I recall in the Bible a reference to "skilled mourners."[47] That's not me. I have spent a lot of years choking back tears. I heard somewhere that if you suffocate the negative it shallows the pool of your passion. Somehow your ability to truly experience joy is diminished. Jesus said in the Beatitudes, "Blessed are you who weep now, For you shall laugh."[48]

I have a theory. Maybe someone more experienced can confirm. Paul says to comfort "with the comfort with which we ourselves are

---

[47] Jeremiah 9:17; Amos 5:16 (NKJV).

[48] Luke 6:21 (NKJV).

comforted by God."⁴⁹ He also says, we don't have to mourn as those who have no hope. Now a "skilled mourner," knows how to mourn. A "skilled mourner" has been comforted by the Comforter. A skilled mourner will know what to do. I have had God talk to me when I cried out to Him. He heard and answered. He gave wisdom, comfort, and counsel. Just like He did for King David. He hasn't changed, even if cultural and custom has.

It is sad that men are cut off by circumstance from something so basically human. Animals don't shed tears for this purpose, just us. If men were allowed to cry out to God in a biblical fashion, they would not be so easily manipulated by a woman's tears because they'd get it. They'd let her process, help her hear from God, AND spot a phony like nobody's business, but the Father's. See, the Father's business is the harvest and the field is ripe with mourning. So many grieving, so unhappy. Tears would be honest, but what good would they do without . . . the Comforter? The prayer has gone out for laborers, but maybe we didn't let the message get buried in the fertile soil of our shared sorrows. Here is what he says about those

---

[49] 2 Corinthians 1:4 (NKJV).

released from captivity, "Those who sow in tears Shall reap in joy. He who continually goes forth weeping, Bearing seed for sowing, Shall DOUBTLESS come again with rejoicing, Bringing his sheaves with him."[50]

    I suppose it does say "him" there doesn't it? Well, guys I am not looking forward to this training much either. But in the day of sorrows, may I not cause drought in my own soul. May I seek His comfort, bear fruit to His glory, and thus my sorrows be redeemed. "Weeping may endure for a night, But joy comes in the morning."[51]

---

[50] **Psalm 126:5-6 (NKJV).**

[51] **Psalm 30:5 (NKJV).**

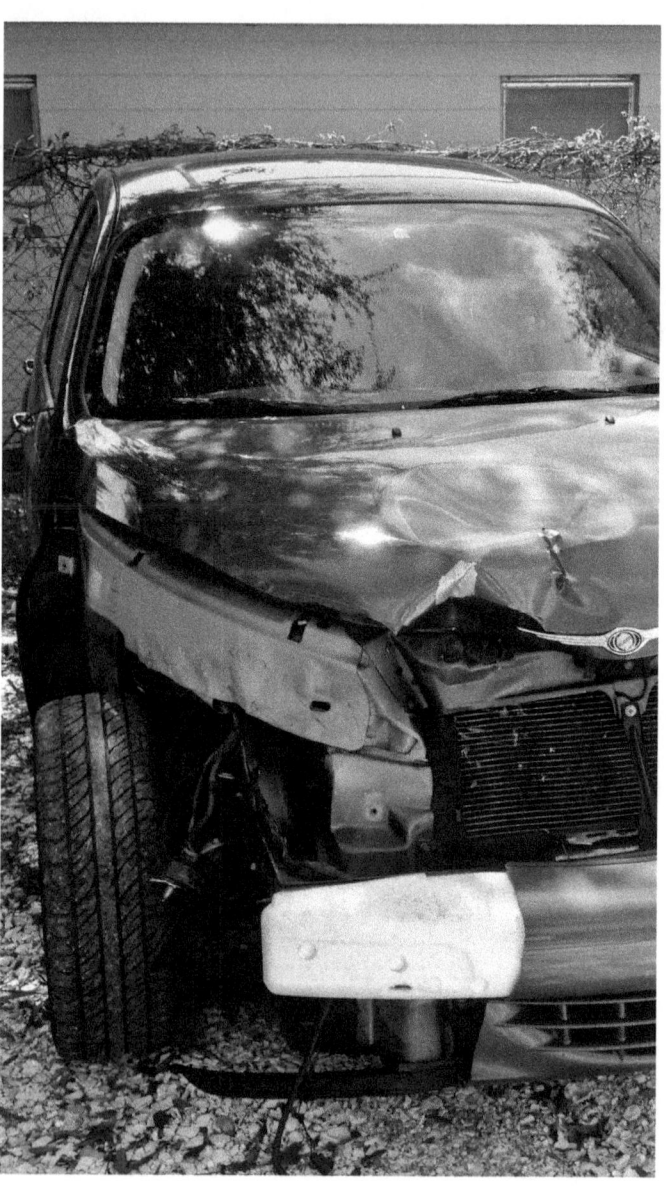

Women Are Vulnerable
Life After the Junkyard

We are the "weaker" sex. I am not even sure what that means, but I never wanted to hear that. Does it mean we are more fragile, hurt easier, deeper, longer? Or is it that we simply, physically are not as muscular? You couldn't have convinced me of that for a moment, even after we arm-wrestled it out. But I am a numbers girl and the data collected by the US military convinced me. I did basic training in my early 20's, slightly older than most of my peers that summer.

There were different standards for men than there were for women in each of the physical fitness tests. I stood there looking at that chart for a long time. I like numbers, I have always liked numbers and the patterns they make. So I noted that sit-ups were pretty close for both by age. But more was expected of men in both the run and the number of pushups to be completed. I studied statistics and I knew how you came up with numbers like this. It would have taken a very extensive sample. Years of America's top athletes, young recruits, and seasoned vets training specifically for these tests. There were some females in our barracks that could outrun almost any male. Most of us were doing good just to qualify for

10 Things I Hated About Being A Woman

our age and sex on this aggregate table. It was hard for me to argue with the data, though there was a time when I would have.

I used to race boys on the playground. I liked to run. I remember a particular time, I couldn't have been more than six or seven. I was chasing or being chased. It was winter and I was bundled up in a big, fluffy coat with the fur around the face. I don't recall the fall, but I still can see the blood. I probably slid 10 feet on my head. My teacher called recess abruptly and ushered me into the bathroom, where she tended my wound. In front of that mirror, I caught my glimpse of the bleeding. There was quite a crowd of curious classmates gathering around the open bathroom door. I was doing my best to choke back tears of shock with the tightly strung tie of my pride. I would not have my weakness noted.

This memory is gentle trauma, an accident, my dome colliding briefly with a slab of blacktop. It is easier to tell this story than what happened at age four in the darkened doorway of an "unmanned" playground. I choose to use a visible wound as example, more sterile, less trigger. I want to label all bad touch as "collision" here, unwanted, uninvited, unpleasant. This can include different kinds of trauma, like injury from an auto accident, falling, or landing on the end of someone's fist.

Life After the Junkyard

They say your body remembers the contact at the cellular level. It registers the pain and holds it. There are people who have been in vehicular incidents that can feel the affects at the point of impact years later. It doesn't matter physically if it is metal and fiberglass, or a fist to the face, or any number of body parts in "collision." Even those most private.

I didn't see it coming. I couldn't prevent it. I couldn't turn away. I couldn't veer out of the trajectory. My wounded body screams at my mind from its lingering memory, a curse: "How could you let this happen? Are you not the master? This wasn't supposed to happen to me! You are supposed to protect me." The sound mind can only reply, "I am not the master. How could I protect you? I'm not the master." Those of us still willing to talk to Him, repeat the refrain to God. "Why me? Why didn't you protect me?" We join the trauma in the song of accusation. So now with all of our being, we charge God of neglect. "Why would You allow this?"

If His answer includes reference to "free will," does that make every man my master? Are we all responsible to protect one another? Must I rely on another's good conscience? Why does his wayward trajectory hold sway over mine? I suppose you can come to this question without ever consulting God. A good lawyer can vindicate the innocent, a good law protect, and a just executioner punish. But who can heal? What can silence the curse bound up in the cells? Who can reconcile the angry member in our own flesh?

You're not ready to hear that yet are you? Still trying to figure out whose side I am on. Maybe some more reason, some stats. I remember the "Take Back the Night Marches" on my college campus. One of the chants was: "No more one in four!" That was the figure calculated illustrating how many women had been raped or molested, 1 in 4, 25%. I hear that number has fallen some in recent years.[52] Perhaps you are wondering if I am part of the 1. Maybe, but I can tell you for sure that I am part of the 4. All women are a part of those numbers. If we're not the 1, we're the 4. One is part of the 4. That's how stats work. We are all part of the selected body of measurement. We are all vulnerable.

With my proclivity toward math, my dad wanted me to be an actuary. I could have been good at that. They crunch numbers for insurance companies by studying the data from accidents and amassing as many cases as possible. They try to isolate variables, making

---

[52] **Rape, Abuse, and Incest National Network,** rainn.org

Life After the Junkyard

it predictable. They are the authors of such questions as: "What age are you? Do you smoke? Do you own your own home?" The odds have been formulated and so have your rates accordingly. But odds don't protect you.

In the Bible, when the enemy was tempting Jesus, the enemy said, "It is written, that God would give His angels charge over you that you might not even stub your toe against a stone."[53] Hardly traumatic right, your toe "colliding" with a rock? He had said this in order to dare Jesus to throw Himself from the highest peak in the city. Now that could be traumatic. Jesus refused, saying, "It is written again, 'You shall not tempt the Lord your God,'"[54] meaning He wasn't gonna do it just to prove it was so.

But on another day in Jerusalem, think about this, the cellular memory of the cat of nine tails across His back. Beaten up to the legal limit until He was near death. Nails, spikes, shards of glass ripping through flesh, flesh that will remember point of impact, not just pain, trauma. He suffered these things, took those 39 stripes, but why? Of all the people ever to walk the Earth, this man was innocent, protected, loved - the darling of

---

[53] **Matthew 4:6 (NLT).**

[54] **Matthew 4:7 (NKJV).**

10 Things I Hated About Being A Woman

Heaven. His steps were ordered by the Lord. Surely no man was His master. No trajectory of craven, mad men could have altered His course.

So what are we supposed to be willing to suffer as He did? Are we to be partakers of what He suffered? Am I just supposed to accept this, this transgression of my boundary, this aggression against my physical being? Jesus bore unjust punishment for your "Why me?", for the accusation of the injury, because you were the wayward trajectory, the missing of the mark.

"What?! How dare you bring up my driving skills? I am obviously not the one to blame." Then who is? If you find someone to hold responsible for poor steering, then know that their path leads here too. That is their punishment on His back for their foolish "I am the master."

It's here or the fiery junkyard for both ya'll. He took the lashes and hung on a tree for all our sins, that there might be healing for everyone. How can He be your God and my God, how can He be when we disagree?

There will be collision (especially if all the pilots turn off their radios, and seek no guidance). Maybe what happened to you was no accident, maybe it was malicious. Maybe they knew exactly what they were doing. That

Life After the Junkyard

malady is not at the point of impact. Your skin will not remember intent. It's your heart that breaks for evil. "If you even harbor hatred in your heart towards your brother, it is as the sin of murder."[55] So, in God's book, harm is done even before the sword is drawn. He is on your side. He is Comforter, Counselor, Prince of Peace.

Hanging on the cross He said, "Father, forgive them, for they do not know what they do."[56] This statement makes little sense given "the law." Of course, people know right and wrong and those responsible should know they crossed the centerline, right? But what if culture repaints the lines? What if culture paints a target on the back of a woman? What if someone told him he is just a complex animal and shouldn't HAVE to control his urges or be in control of his own vehicle? Maybe that looks like oppression to him. Maybe the control he is looking for isn't of his own body, but to lord it over another.

Jesus said, "You know that the rulers in this world lord it over their people, and officials flaunt their authority over those under

---

[55] I John 3:15 (NKJV).

[56] Luke 23:34 (NKJV).

them. But among you it will be different."[57] He said this to give us hope. Throughout the Bible, there are stories of people who cried out to God because of their oppression . . . and He heard them. You need to know that God is for you and He hears you, I'd call that "faith" any day. But this is not a silent faith. Pastor Phil Derstine says of facing Giants: "Faith SEES, faith SPEAKS, and faith ACTS."[58] You've got to SEE something deeper than your problem. There is something wrong here and you are a witness of it. Cry up! And then cry out! These pages have been penned through prayer and are inspired by a Spirit of Holiness. I can tell you there is nothing more empowering than purpose.

    Now I like a good girl "kicks butt" movie as well as the next person. But there has got to be something more glorious that we can do rather than beat somebody up. I don't know what He is calling you to do. But there is something personal, tailor made, that redeems - buys back - all the accidents you have been involved in. There will be collision, but there will be restoration, not by the power that struck His back or hung Him on the cross, but

---

[57] Matthew 20:25-26 (NLT).

[58] Phil Derstine, Purpose for Life Devotional. www.philderstine.com

Life After the Junkyard

by the power that resurrected Him. So be healed in Jesus name.

Epilogue
Reign Shelter

  I have purposefully over extended stereotypes here. The truth is we are not all made the same and you don't need me to tell you that or confirm it. Much of what I label as character strengths of a woman are present in men too. I am not the designer and don't claim to be. I am here as ambassador, working toward reconciliation.[59]

  The battle of the sexes will not end by our roaring. It will only raise up lion tamers. Debunking stereotypes is like shadow boxing. It can lead us deeper into struggle with ourselves and only prepare us to become champions of oppression. How can we be the Biblical bride, when her role is so self-loathing? How we treat each other, recognize ourselves as made second, pulled out of the second Adam, part of Him but not Him, it changes what it means to be His bride. It is a great mystery. Let us unravel it together as men and women, one flesh, one man.

  I didn't say much about marriage here, but feel I should. Paul said, "Wives, submit yourselves unto your own husbands, as unto

---

[59] 2 Corinthians 5:20 (NIV).

the Lord."[60] I know how submission sounds, but he also says to the husbands, "Husbands, love your wives, just as Christ loved the church and gave himself up for her."[61] At one point, that would have made me toss the whole book and run from marriage. But listen, God knows men and women, and how He has made them. Is it not one of the hardest things for a woman to do to TRUST? God is not advocating slavery here. He hates oppression. He brought his people out of slavery. So how does a free woman submit freely? She trusts.

A man is in training in marriage too. He is to understand that authority given to him and how to carry it. He is to carry it in a way that honors the God whose authority he is submitted to as Lord. Jesus said, "For my yoke is easy, my burden is light."[62] He "gave himself up for her" is not tyranny. That is why how you see God as an author, as an "authority" really matters. Let me rehearse with you His story of authoritarianism.

God brought them out of slavery through Moses. Moses was governing disputes and settling differences all day. His

---

[60] **Ephesians 5:22 (KJV).**

[61] **Ephesians 5:25 (NIV).**

[62] **Matthew 11:30 (NIV).**

Reign Shelter

father-in-law suggested he train some people to help him with smaller matters, men who feared God. It was after that God gave the ten commandments at Mount Sinai. If you think about it, it makes sense to put something in writing for training purposes, right? God knows these are a stiff-necked people. While Moses is gone, they pool their money, make their own God, and have an orgy. Moses breaks the covenant on the rocks, but begs God not to kill them all and start over. Guess that is where we start with the accusations against God, the death penalty. Seems like everything is the death penalty. You kill somebody on purpose, you die. If it is on accident, there is a way of escape, but adultery - you die. Kidnapping - you die. Curse your mother and father - you die. Overall the law makes sense and is good. It labels the do's and don'ts like a help-me-judge manual. But it is a blood law. Sacrifice must be made for infraction. It is a law that does not draw the line lightly without conviction. It is purely "just."

Enter Jesus. He is the perfect sacrifice, planned from the beginning, the fulfillment of the law. You asked for a king and you will cry out for relief from that king.[63] God sent His Son and He gave Himself to satisfy your death

---

[63] **1 Samuel 8:7-18 (NIV).**

penalty. He embodied the law, lived the law, in Spirit and in truth, trustworthy. He dealt mercy everywhere He went, healing what had been cursed. The law in stone had become a weapon of man's destruction, but written in flesh, He become their redemption. This is the new covenant: "I will put my law in their minds and write it on their hearts. I will be their God, and they will be my people. No longer will a man teach his neighbor, or a man his brother, saying, 'Know the Lord,' because they will all know me, from the least of them to the greatest," declares the Lord. "For I will forgive their wickedness and will remember their sins no more."[64] This is where the two become one flesh, the Word written on our hearts, posted on the doorway of our life's blood, that the wrath of God would pass over us. His sacrifice making us new creatures, but not by force, nor by power, but ... "by my Spirit," says the Lord Almighty.[65]

So I am not going to say, "Know your God," but rather invite Him in as Lord. He won't take more than you are willing to give, and by willing I mean enthusiastically being directed from the heart. Because the Bible says,

---

[64] **Jeremiah 31:33-34 (NIV).**

[65] **Zechariah 4:6 (NIV).**

Reign Shelter

He is enthroned in our praises,[66] and that "He loves a cheerful giver."[67] He is not looking for auto-matrons to do His bidding. He wants to build a home together with His bride.

---

[66] Psalm 22:3 (NKJV).

[67] 2 Corinthians 9:7b (NKJV).

About the Author

Christie Nafziger is a graduate of the Institute of Ministry, an "Able Minister" through Gospel Crusade. She also is an alumnus of Indiana University, home of the Kinsey Institute, where she earned a Bachelor of Science in Mathematics Education. She is married to photographer Tyler Nafziger, who heads their business "Resounding Love Media." The two labor together on selective photo and video projects from their home base in Florida.

Photos pages 6 & 88: Al Gordon Photography (www.algordonphoto.com)

Photos pages 12, 20, 28, 36, 50, 58, 66, & 72: Tyler Nafziger, Resounding Love Media (www.resoundinglovemedia.com)

www.ingramcontent.com/pod-product-compliance
Lightning Source LLC
Chambersburg PA
CBHW071313040426
42444CB00009B/2005